# Introduction

What do you get when you give a group of quilt designers four rulers, a mission and a request for creativity? The answer is exceptional ideas and fantastic patterns that show off their impressive talents.

Most quilters have an overabundance of rulers lying around their sewing rooms stuffed in boxes and drawers. Many were purchased for a particular pattern or project and then forgotten. Rulers are exceptional tools if you actually use them. The problem with rulers is that once purchased and used for the project intended, they are quickly forgotten unless there are support patterns available to keep you using the rulers.

In *Quilts Made With Rulers* you will find not only the patterns to support four rulers, but also lots of guidance on how to use them. You will also discover tips and tricks to stretch your imagination and help you explore some of the many ways they can be used. Think of your rulers as tools to make your quilting better and easier.

*Quilts Made With Rulers* is your go-to book for the 120-Degree Triangle, the 45-Degree Diamond, the Double Wedding Ring Single Arc and the Flying Geese rulers. It's an idea book with knowledge to expand how you use them. Take the plunge and step outside the box with fun and creative quilt designs made easy with these rulers.

Each project in this book has a highlighted icon of the ruler used at the top of the pattern page for easy reference. Just glance at the icon and instantly know which ruler you will need to use. We hope you try them all.

# Table of Contents

## Flying Geese Ruler

## 120-Degree Triangle Ruler

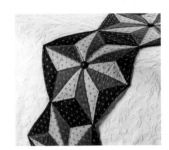

## 45-Degree Diamond Ruler

## Double Wedding Ring Single Arc Ruler

# General Instructions for Using EZ Rulers

Each of the four rulers used in this book can make the construction of your quilts easier by taking advantage of rotary-cutting techniques and eliminating some of the math involved in figuring piece sizes.

Follow the simple steps presented here to use each of these rulers or watch a how-to video provided through AnniesCraftStore.com.

## EZ Quilting® Flying Geese Ruler

This flying geese ruler allows you to cut flying geese units from 1½" x 3" finished up to 6" x 12" finished. When using these rulers the flying geese units are measured by their height and width.

A flying geese unit is comprised of two parts: the center triangle, also referred to as the "goose" or "body," and the side triangles or "wings" which are mirror images of each other.

Both sides of the Flying Geese ruler are used to cut these parts. Side A of the ruler, with magenta pink lines, is used to cut the center triangle. Side B, with aqua green lines, is used to cut the side triangles.

## To Cut Flying Geese Units

**1.** Determine desired finished size of unit. On ruler Side A, locate finished size and follow the line to indicated width of fabric strip needed.

**2.** Cut fabric strips to indicated width for both center and side triangles.

**3.** To cut center triangle, align the top of the Side A with the top edge of fabric strip. The bottom of the strip will align with the corresponding width measurement on the ruler.

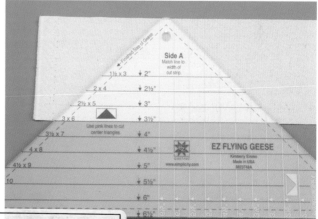

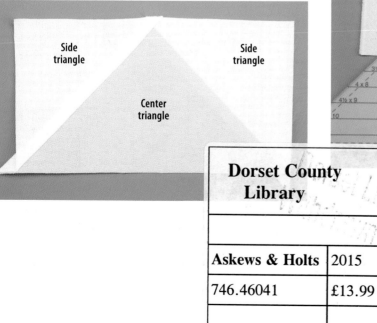

**4.** Cut along both sides of the ruler using a rotary cutter.

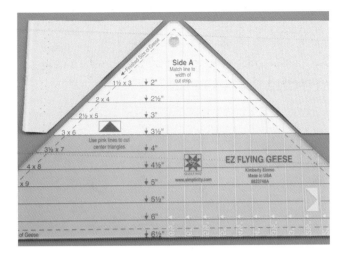

**5.** Rotate the ruler 180 degrees and align with the diagonally cut edge of the fabric and the top and bottom fabric edges. Make next cut.

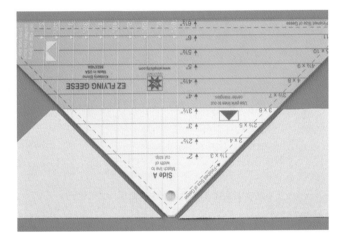

**6.** Continue rotating the ruler and cutting center triangles along the fabric strip.

**7.** To cut the side triangles, fold the fabric strip right side together and trim selvages.

**8.** Align the top of the ruler with the top edge of the fabric strip using ruler Side B. The bottom of the strip will align with the corresponding width measurement on the ruler.

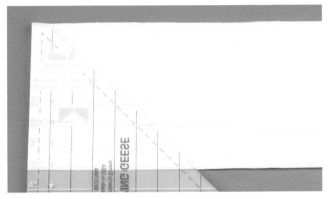

**9.** Using a rotary cutter, cut through both layers to create the mirror-image side triangles.

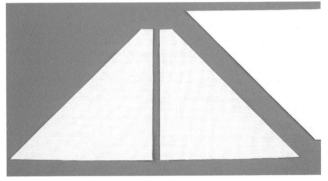

**10.** Rotate the ruler 180 degrees and align with the diagonally cut edge of the fabric as well as the strip top and bottom; make next cut.

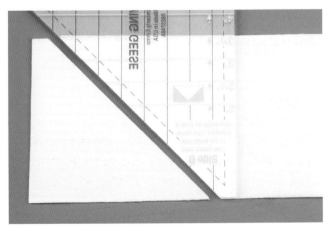

**11.** Continue rotating the ruler and cutting side triangles along the fabric strip.

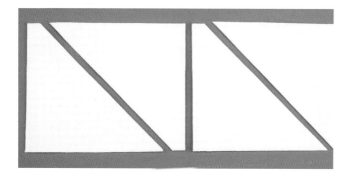

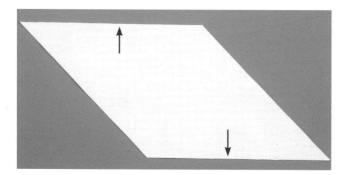

## EZ Quilting® 45-Degree Diamond Ruler

This versatile ruler allows you to cut diamond shapes ranging from 1" finished height to 3½" finished height.

When using this ruler, the height of a diamond is measured from flat side to flat side, indicated by the red arrows, **NOT** tip to tip.

The dashed lines on the ruler indicate the finished size of each diamond and the solid lines are used for lining up with the fabric for cutting.

### Designer's Tip

*Two sides of the diamond will have bias edges and will need to be handled with care to avoid stretching. Applying spray starch to the strips and ironing dry before cutting will make the pieces easier to handle.*

## To Cut 45-Degree Diamonds

**1.** Cut a fabric width strip according to the measurements on the ruler based on the finished size of diamond desired.

**2.** Position ruler on one end of fabric and trim to establish a 45-degree angle.

**3.** Position the ruler with the solid lines for the desired finished size of the diamond being cut along cut edges of fabric strip to make the final cut for the diamond.

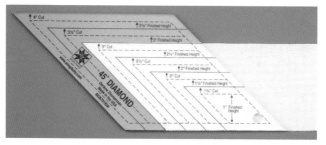

**4.** Continue cutting diamonds along length of fabric strip.

## EZ Quilting® 120-Degree Triangle Ruler

The 120-Degree Triangle ruler allows you to cut triangle shapes that range from 1" finished height to 6" finished height. This ruler will cut both 120-degree full triangles and 120-degree half triangles.

The height of the triangle is measured from the top point to the base of the triangle.

The angle formed at the top point is 120 degrees.

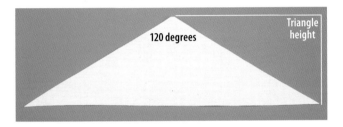

The lines on the ruler indicate the width of fabric strip from which you are cutting the triangles. To determine the finished size, subtract ½" for the seam allowances.

### To Cut 120-Degree Full Triangles

**1.** Cut a fabric strip the width of the finished triangle plus ½".

**2.** Fold the fabric over, right sides together, the width of the triangle to be cut . Align the ruler dashed seamline on the fold.

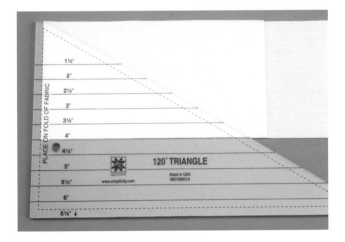

**3.** Cut along the angle.

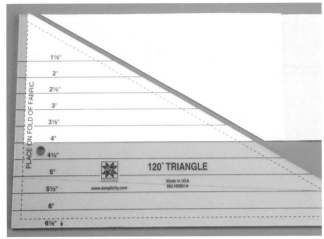

**4.** Fold the fabric again right sides together and rotate the ruler so the tip is facing down. Align ruler dashed seamline on the fold.

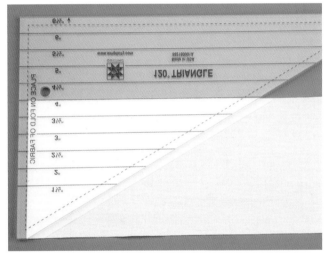

**5.** Cut along the angle.

**6.** Continue folding the fabric and rotating the ruler to cut more triangles

## To Cut 120-Degree Half Triangles

**1.** Cut a fabric strip the width of the finished triangle plus ½".

**2.** Align the outer edge of the ruler with the fabric edge.

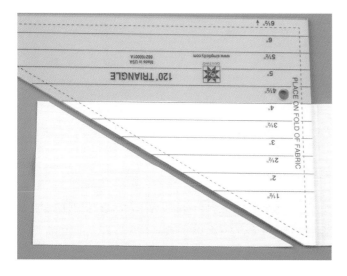

**3.** Cut along the angle.

**4.** Rotate the ruler so the tip is facing down. Align ruler with edges of fabric strip.

**5.** Cut along the angle.

**6.** Continue rotating the ruler to cut more triangles.

**7.** To cut mirror-image triangles, cut on the reverse side of the fabric.

## EZ Quilting® Double Wedding Ring Single Arc Ruler

Typically this ruler is used in conjunction with the EZ Quilting Double Wedding Ring Template Set where the Single Arc ruler replaces the smaller individual pieces of the arc. However, on its own, the ruler works beautifully to create gentle curved pieces which can be pieced into other patterns or used for appliqué.

## To Cut Single Arcs

Place the ruler on the fabric and cut around it.

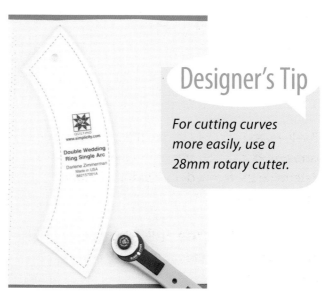

### Designer's Tip

*For cutting curves more easily, use a 28mm rotary cutter.*

In order to minimize fabric waste, cut an 11" by fabric width strip and nest the arcs as close to together as possible. ●

# Candy Hearts

Designed & Quilted by Julie Weaver

Turn Flying Geese blocks into gorgeous vintage hearts the easy way. This would make the perfect baby shower gift.

## Skill Level
Confident Beginner

## Finished Size
Quilt Size: 42" x 50"
Block Size: 8" x 8"
Number of Blocks: 20

## Materials
- ⅓ yard each 20 1930s reproduction prints
- 1¼ yards white solid
- Backing to size
- Batting to size
- Thread
- Flying Geese ruler by EZ Quilting
- Basic sewing tools and supplies

## Project Notes
Read all instructions before beginning this project.

Stitch right sides together using a ¼" seam allowance unless otherwise specified.

Refer to a favorite quilting guide for specific techniques.

Materials and cutting lists assume 40" of usable fabric width.

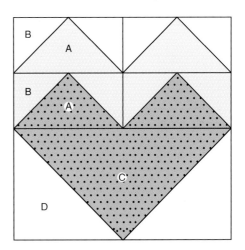

**Candy Hearts**
8" x 8" Finished Block
Make 20

## Cutting
Refer to General Instructions for Flying Geese ruler on page 3 for specific cutting instructions of flying geese "bodies" (center triangles) and "wings" (side triangles).

## From 1930s reproduction prints:
Select 4 prints to use for the cornerstones in the pieced border; from each of these prints:

- Cut 1 (4½" by fabric width) strip.
    Subcut strip into 1 (3½") K square and 1 C center triangle, aligning Flying Geese ruler 4½" line with long edge of fabric.

- Trim remainder of strip to 2" wide.
  Subcut strip into 5 (2" x 3½") G rectangles.
  Reserve 2½" wide strip for binding.
- Cut 1 (2½" by fabric width) strip.
  Subcut strip into 4 A center triangles and 4 B side triangles, aligning Flying Geese ruler 2½" line with long edge of fabric.

## From each of remaining 16 prints:

- Cut 1 (4½" by fabric width) strip.
  Subcut strip into 1 C center triangle, aligning Flying Geese ruler 4½" line with long edge of fabric.
- Trim remainder of strip to 2" wide.
  Subcut strip into 5 (2" x 3½") G rectangles.
  Reserve 2½" wide strip for binding.
- Cut 1 (2½" by fabric width) strip.
  Subcut strip into 4 A center triangles and 4 B side triangles, aligning Flying Geese ruler 2½" line with long edge of fabric.

### Designer's Tip

*Keep all the cuts from each print together in separate stacks. This makes it easy to pair the pieces from two different prints together to make each block.*

## From white solid:

- Cut 3 (4½" by fabric width) strips.
  Subcut strips into 40 D "wing" triangles, aligning Flying Geese ruler 4½" line with long edge of fabric.
- Cut 4 (2½" by fabric width) strips.
  Subcut strips into 80 B "wing" triangles, aligning Flying Geese ruler 2½" line with long edge of fabric.
- Cut 4 (1½" by fabric width) E/F strips.
- Cut 5 (1½" by fabric width) H/I strips.

## Completing the Blocks

**1.** For one block select two A and one C triangle of the same print, two A and four B triangles of the same print, and four B and two D triangles of white.

### Designer's Tip

*After all of the triangles have been selected for each block, you can easily store them in zip-top plastic bags to keep each block together.*

**2.** Referring to the block drawing for color placement, sew two white B triangles onto each side of an A triangle as shown in Figure 1; press toward the A triangle. Repeat with the remaining same-fabric A triangle to make two upper flying geese units.

Make 2

**Figure 1**

**3.** Using the same print as the A triangle in step 2, sew two print B triangles onto each side of a different-print A triangle as shown in Figure 2; press toward B triangles. Repeat to make two lower flying geese units.

Make 2

**Figure 2**

**4.** Using the same print as the A center triangle in step 3, sew two D triangles onto each side of the C triangle to make a C-D unit as shown in Figure 3; press toward the C triangle.

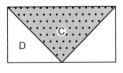

**Figure 3**

**5.** Referring to the Block Diagram, sew two upper flying geese units together to form the top row and two lower flying geese units together to form the center row.

**6.** Sew the top and center rows and the C-D unit together to complete one block.

**7.** Repeat steps 1–6 to make a total of 20 Candy Hearts blocks.

## Completing the Quilt

**1.** Arrange and join four Candy Hearts blocks to make a row as shown in the Assembly Diagram; press. Repeat to make five rows, pressing seams in opposite directions in adjacent rows.

**2.** Join the rows to complete the quilt center; press.

**3.** Join the E/F strips on the short ends to make a long strip; press. Subcut strip into two (1½" x 40½") E strips and two (1½" x 34½") F strips.

**4.** Sew E strips to the opposite long sides of the quilt center and F strips to the top and bottom; press seams toward strips.

**5.** Sew 28 G rectangles together on the long sides to create a side border strip. Repeat to make two side border strips.

> ### Designer's Tip
> If the pieced borders don't measure the same length as the quilt center, you can easily adjust the width of the seam allowance to make the border shorter or longer as needed.

**6.** Sew side border strips to opposite long sides of quilt center, press towards the center.

**7.** Sew 22 G rectangles together on the long sides to create a top/bottom border. Repeat to make a second top/bottom border.

**8.** Sew K squares onto each end of the top/bottom borders. Press seams toward K.

**9.** Sew top/bottom borders in place; press toward the quilt center.

**10.** Join the H/I strips on the short ends to make a long strip; press. Subcut strip into two (1½" x 48½") I strips and two (1½" x 42½") H strips.

**11.** Sew H strips to the opposite long sides of the quilt center and I strips to the top and bottom; press seams toward strips.

**12.** Sandwich the batting between the pieced top and a prepared backing piece; baste layers together. Quilt as desired.

**13.** When quilting is complete, remove basting, and trim batting and backing fabric even with raw edges of the pieced top.

**14.** Prepare binding by sewing reserved binding strips together on the short ends to total 194 inches. Stitch to quilt front edges, matching raw edges, mitering corners and overlapping ends. Fold binding to back side and stitch in place to finish. ●

*"This project combines two of my favorites—hearts and pieced borders. Reproduction prints always give me inspiration, and the Flying Geese ruler makes the blocks easy, easy, easy!" —Julie Weaver*

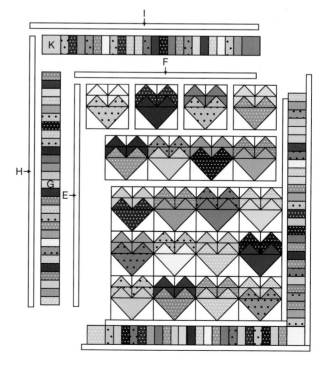

**Candy Hearts**
Assembly Diagram 42" x 50"

# On a Wild Goose Chase

Design by Chris Malone
Quilted by Jean McDaniel

Make this bright and cheerful quilt for a young person in your life. This project is a great way to add color to a room while using up your stash.

## Skill Level
Confident Beginner

## Finished Size
Quilt Size: 48" x 64"
Block Size: 16" x 16"
Number of Blocks: 12

## Materials
- ¼ yard or fat quarter of 12 dark-color prints or tonals
- ¼ yard or fat quarter of 12 light-color prints or tonals to coordinate with dark-color prints or tonals
- ½ yard coordinating print
- 2¼ yards white tonal
- Backing to size
- Batting to size
- Thread
- Flying Geese ruler by EZ Quilting
- Basic sewing tools and supplies

## Project Notes
Read all instructions before beginning this project.

Stitch right sides together using a ¼" seam allowance unless otherwise specified.

Refer to a favorite quilting guide for specific techniques.

Materials and cutting lists assume 40" of usable fabric width.

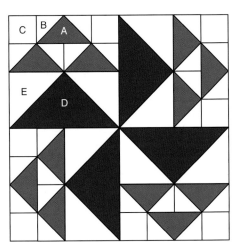

**Wild Geese**
16" x 16" Finished Block
Make 12

## Cutting
Refer to General Instructions for Flying Geese ruler on page 3 for specific cutting instructions of flying geese "bodies" or center triangles and "wings" or side triangles.

### From each dark-color print or tonal:
- Cut 1 (4½" by fabric width) strip or 2 (4½" x 18") strips from fat quarter.
  Subcut strip(s) into 4 large D triangles, lining up the 4½" line on ruler with the long edge of fabric.

### From each light-color print or tonal:
- Cut 1 (2½" by fabric width) strip or 3 (2½" x 18") strips from fat quarter.
  Subcut strip(s) into 12 small A center triangles, lining up the 2½" line on ruler with the edge of fabric.

## From coordinating print:
- Cut 6 (2¼" by fabric width) binding strips.

## From white tonal:
- Cut 6 (4½" by fabric width) strips.
  Subcut strips into 48 mirror-image E triangle pairs, lining up the 4½" line on ruler with the bottom long edge of fabric.
- Cut 18 (2½" by fabric width) strips.
  Subcut 12 strips into 144 mirror-image B triangle pairs, lining up the 2½" line on ruler with the bottom long edge of fabric.
  Subcut the remaining 6 strips into 96 (2½") C squares.

### Designer's Tip

When using the Flying Geese ruler to cut B shapes from folded or layered strips, be sure the strips are like-sides facing (right sides together or wrong sides together) so you end up with mirror images.

Follow the instructions on page 3 to flip the ruler up and down as you cut across the strips.

## Completing the Blocks

**1.** Each block requires four same-fabric D triangles, 12 coordinating same-fabric A triangles, four mirror-image pairs of E triangles, 12 mirror-image pairs of B triangles and eight C squares.

**2.** Select one color set and sew one B triangle to the left side of an A triangle as shown in Figure 1; press seam toward B. Stitch a mirror-image B triangle to right side of A, again referring to Figure 1; press seam toward B.

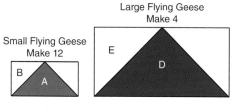

**Figure 1**

**3.** Repeat step 2 with remaining small A and B triangles and with D and E triangles to make 12 small flying geese units and four large flying geese units referring to Figure 2.

**Figure 2**

**4.** Stitch two small flying geese units together on one short side (Figure 3); press seam open. Repeat to make a total of four double units.

Make 4

**Figure 3**

**5.** Stitch a C square to each side of the remaining four small flying geese units (Figure 4); press seams toward C.

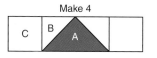
Make 4

**Figure 4**

**6.** Stitch a C-B-A row to the top of each double unit to make a stacked unit (Figure 5); press seam open.

Make 4

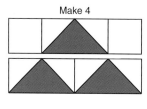

**Figure 5**

**7.** Stitch a stacked unit to the top edge of a large flying geese unit to make a quarter block unit (Figure 6); press seams open.

Make 4

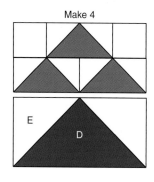

**Figure 6**

**8.** Repeat steps 1–7 with remaining color set pieces to make a total of four matching quarter block units.

**9.** Referring to the block diagram, arrange the four quarter units, rotating each unit so the D triangles form a pinwheel in the block center.

**10.** Stitch the quarter block units together in rows and then stitch rows together. Refer to Spinning Centers to Reduce Bulk on page 17 for pressing instructions to avoid bulk at the block center.

**11.** Repeat steps 1–10 to make a total of 12 Wild Geese blocks each a different color combination referring to the Assembly Diagram.

*Designer's Tip*

*In a quilt like this with all the points and angles, accuracy in cutting, sewing and pressing is especially important for good results.*

## Completing the Quilt

**1.** Arrange the blocks into four rows of three blocks each. Stitch the blocks together in rows as arranged, pressing seams in adjacent rows in the opposite directions. Stitch rows together to complete the quilt top referring again to the Assembly Diagram.

**2.** Sandwich the batting between the pieced top and a prepared backing piece; baste layers together. Quilt as desired.

**3.** When quilting is complete, remove basting, and trim batting and backing fabric even with raw edges of the pieced top.

**4.** Prepare binding and stitch to quilt front edges, matching raw edges, mitering corners and overlapping ends. Fold binding to back side and stitch in place to finish. ●

*"Don't we all have days that resemble this quilt? One idea, one task points to another and another, and by evening we feel like we have been on a wild goose chase all day long!" —Chris Malone*

**On a Wild Goose Chase**
Assembly Diagram 48" x 64"

**On a Wild Goose Chase**
Alternative Size Option
Assembly Diagram 64" x 80"
Make 20 blocks and stitch into 5 rows
of 4 blocks each to make a twin-size quilt.

# Spinning Centers to Reduce Bulk

When sewing a block where numerous points meet together, there can be a lot of bulk in the seam allowance on the wrong side of the fabric. This extra bulk prohibits the block from lying flat when pressed. One option is to trim the points off, thus reducing the amount of fabric in the seam allowance. Another option is to "spin" the center of the seam allowances, thus distributing the bulk more evenly.

**1.** Stitch the block as usual nesting seams at any intersection (Photo A).

Photo A

**2.** Before pressing, remove approximately three stitches in the seam allowance from each side of the previously sewn seams (Photo B).

Photo B

**3.** Place the block on a pressing board right side down (Photo C).

Photo C

**4.** With your fingers, push the top seam to the right and the bottom seam to the left. This will result in the seam allowances spinning in a clockwise direction (Photo D).

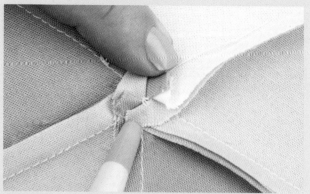

Photo D

**5.** The center will pop open and the seam allowances will swirl around the center of the block (Photo E).

Photo E

**6.** Press with an iron to flatten the seam allowances in place (Photo F).

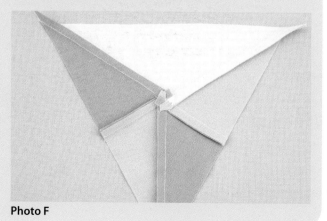

Photo F

# Shadows

### Designed & Quilted by Julie Weaver

This table topper is the perfect project to complete on a rainy afternoon or when time is at a premium. It would make a great gift.

## Skill Level
Confident Beginner

## Finished Size
Topper Size: 27" x 27"
Block Sizes: 3" x 6" and 3" x 3" finished
Number of Blocks: 16 and 4

## Materials
- ⅛ yard white solid
- ⅛ yard navy print 1
- ¼ yard green print
- ⅜ yard white floral print
- ½ yard red print
- ½ yard navy print 2
- Flying Geese ruler by EZ Quilting
- Thread
- Batting to size
- Backing to size
- Basic sewing tools and supplies

## Project Notes
Read all instructions before beginning this project.

Stitch right sides together using a ¼" seam allowance unless otherwise specified.

Refer to a favorite quilting guide for specific techniques.

Materials and cutting lists assume 40" of usable fabric width.

**Half Square**
3" x 3" Finished Block
Make 4

**Flying Geese**
3" x 6" Finished Block
Make 16

## Cutting
Refer to General Instructions for flying geese ruler on page 3 for specific cutting instructions of flying geese "bodies" (center triangles) and "wings" (side triangles).

### From white solid:
- Cut 1 (3⅞" by fabric width) strip.
    Subcut strip into 2 (3⅞") A squares.
- Trim remainder of strip to 3½" wide.
    Subcut 16 C side triangles lining up the 3½" line of the ruler with the long edge of fabric.

### From navy print 1:
- Cut 1 (3½" by fabric width) strip.
    Subcut strip into 4 D center triangles.

### Designer's Tip
*I've always used the sew-and-flip method to make Flying Geese blocks. Using this ruler definitely cuts down on waste.*

## From green print:
- Cut 1 (3½" by fabric width) strip.
  Subcut strip into 4 D center triangles.
- Cut 1 (3½" by fabric width) strip.
  Subcut strip into 8 C side triangles lining up the 3½" line on the ruler with the long edge of fabric.

## From white floral print:
- Cut 4 (2" by fabric width) strips.
  Subcut strips into 2 each 2" x 22½" I and 2" x 24½" J borders.

## From red print:
- Cut 1 (3⅞" by fabric width) strip.
  Subcut strip into 2 (3⅞") B squares.
- Trim remainder of strip to 3½" wide.
  Subcut strip into 16 C side triangles lining up the 3½" line of the ruler with the long edge of fabric.
  Unfold trimmed strip and subcut 8 D center triangles.
- Cut 1 (3½" by fabric width) strip.
  Subcut strip into 8 C side triangles lining up the 3½" line on the ruler with the long edge of fabric.
- Cut 4 (1½" by fabric width) strips.
  Subcut strips into 2 each 1½" x 20½" G and 1½" x 22½" H borders.

## From navy print 2:
- Cut 2 (1½" by fabric width) strips.
  Subcut strips into 2 each 1½" x 18½" E and 1½" x 20½" F borders.
- Cut 4 (1½" by fabric width) strips.
  Subcut strips into 2 each 1½" x 25½" K and 1½" x 27½" L borders.

### Designer's Tip
*Follow the manufacturer's included instructions (or refer to page 3) to cut and sew the triangles. I was pleasantly surprised at how easy the blocks were to make!*

## Completing the Half Square Blocks
**1.** Draw a diagonal line on wrong side of both A squares.

**2.** Layer one A square right sides together with a B square and stitch ¼" on either side of drawn line (Figure 1a). Cut apart on drawn line (Figure 1b).

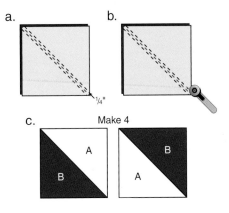

**Figure 1**

**3.** Press seam allowance toward B. Repeat step 2 to make four A-B Half Square blocks (Figure 1c).

### Designer's Tip
*Press, press, press as you go! Conscientious pressing will also make assembly much easier!*

## Completing the Flying Geese Blocks
**1.** Position and stitch a white solid C triangle on both angled edges of a red print D triangle to complete a Flying Geese block (Figure 2). Press seams toward D.

**Figure 2**

**2.** Repeat step 1 to make eight red print/white solid C-D Flying Geese blocks (Figure 3). Repeat step 1 with red print C and green print D triangles, and with green print C and navy print 1 D triangles to make four of each color combination.

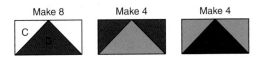

**Figure 3**

## Completing the Quilt Center

**1.** Stitch two each Half Square blocks and red/white Flying Geese blocks together in a row referring to Figure 4. Repeat to make two top/bottom rows.

Top/Bottom Row
Make 2

**Figure 4**

**2.** Stitch a red/green Flying Geese block to a green/navy Flying Geese block, matching the green print edges (Figure 5). Repeat to make four double units.

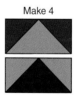

Make 4

**Figure 5**

**3.** Stitch two red/white Flying Geese blocks and two double units together referring to Figure 6 for placement. Press seams to avoid bulk. Repeat to make a second center row.

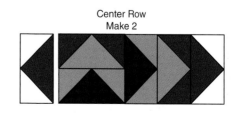

Center Row
Make 2

**Figure 6**

**4.** Arrange and stitch rows together referring to the Assembly Diagram to complete the quilt center. Press seams open to avoid bulk.

**5.** Stitch borders to completed quilt center in alphabetical order and stitching first the side borders and then the top and bottom borders referring to the Assembly Diagram. Press seams toward borders.

## Completing the Quilt

**1.** Sandwich the batting between the pieced top and a prepared backing piece; baste layers together. Quilt as desired.

**2.** When quilting is complete, remove basting, and trim batting and backing fabric even with raw edges of the pieced top.

**3.** Prepare binding and stitch to quilt front edges, matching raw edges, mitering corners and overlapping ends. Fold binding to back side and stitch in place to finish. ●

**Shadows**
Assembly Diagram 27" x 27"

*"The challenge of the ruler was the inspiration for this quilt. So many designs, both traditional and contemporary, can be created from the Flying Geese block. This block is so versatile that it's become one of my favorites. I've always made these blocks using the sew-and-flip method, but I was inspired to try something a little different because of the ruler challenge!"* —Julie Weaver

# Patriotic Pinwheels

Designed & Quilted by Holly Daniels

Make this spinning pinwheel using a 120-degree triangle ruler and half-block construction. Cutting triangles with two colors is amazingly easy with this ruler.

## Skill Level
Advanced

## Finished Size
Quilt Size: 52" x 60"
Block Size: 11½" x 13½"
Number of Blocks: 16

## Materials
- ¼ yard each 8 different red prints and 8 different blue prints
- 1 yard dark blue print
- 1⅓ yards dark tan print
- 2⅛ yards light tan tonal
- Backing to size
- Batting to size
- Thread
- 120-Degree Triangle ruler by EZ Quilting
- Basic sewing tools and supplies

## Project Notes
Read all instructions before beginning this project.

Stitch right sides together using a ¼" seam allowance unless otherwise specified.

Refer to a favorite quilting guide for specific techniques.

Materials and cutting lists assume 40" of usable fabric width.

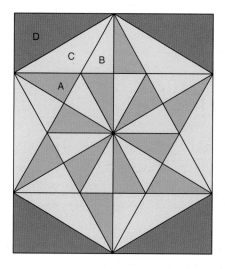

**Blue Pinwheel**
11½" x 13½" Finished Block
Make 8

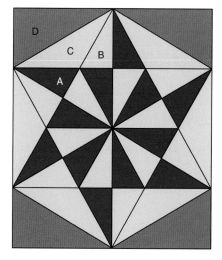

**Red Pinwheel**
11½" x 13½" Finished Block
Make 8

## Cutting

Refer to General Instructions for 120-Degree Triangle ruler on page 6 for specific cutting instructions.

### From each red & blue print:
- Cut 1 (5" x 16") A rectangles.

### From dark blue print:
- Cut 6 (2" by fabric width) G/H strips.
- Cut 6 (2½" by fabric width) binding strips.

### From dark tan print:
- Cut 7 (4" by fabric width) strips.
  Subcut strips into 32 D triangles and 32 DR reversed triangles lining up raw edge of fabric with edge of ruler.
- Cut 6 (2" by fabric width) E/F strips.

### From light tan tonal:
- Cut 2 (16" by fabric width) strips.
  Subcut strips into 16 (5" x 16") B rectangles.
- Cut 14 (2½" by fabric width) strips.
  Subcut strips into 96 C triangles with dashed line on ruler aligned with folded edge of fabric.

## Completing the Blocks

**1.** Pair each A rectangle with a B rectangle. With right sides together, sew ¼" from each side of strip (Figure 1). Press to set seams.

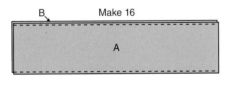

**Figure 1**

**2.** Cut each strip into six 2½" x 5" strips.

**3.** With red or blue fabric on top, align the dotted line on short side of the 120-Degree Triangle ruler with the seam line on the strip set as shown in Figure 2a and cut diagonally into two triangles. Open up the A-B units (Figure 2b) and carefully press seams toward A.

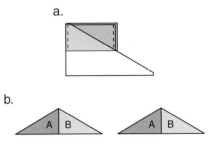

**Figure 2**

**4.** Repeat step 3 with each of the sewn strips sets to make a total of 12 A-B units from each of the 16 red and blue prints.

**5.** Following the color placement and orientation as shown in Figure 3 and referring to Stitching a Set-In or Y-Seam on page 27, sew two same-fabric A-B units and one C triangle together using a set-in seam to assemble a wedge. Repeat to make six wedges.

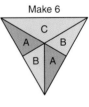

**Figure 3**

**6.** Sew three wedges together to form a half-hexagon (Figure 4). Repeat to make a second half-hexagon.

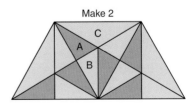

**Figure 4**

**7.** Sew the two half-hexagons together to form a hexagon.

**8.** Sew D triangles and reverse D triangles onto four sides of each hexagon to complete one block as shown in Figure 5.

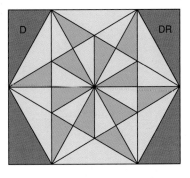

**Figure 5**

**9.** Repeat steps 5–8 to complete a block in each of the different red and blue prints.

## Completing the Quilt

**1.** Alternating red and blue blocks as shown in the Assembly Diagram, sew four blocks together to form a row; press rows in opposite directions. Repeat to make four rows.

**2.** Following color placement of blocks in the Assembly Diagram, sew rows together to complete the quilt center; press.

**3.** Join the E/F strips on the short ends to make a long strip; press. Subcut strip into two 2" x 54½" E strips and two 2" x 49½" F strips.

**4.** Sew the E strips to opposite sides and F strips to top and bottom of the quilt center. Press seams toward the strips.

**5.** Join the G/H strips on the short ends to make a long strip; press. Subcut strip into two 2" x 57½" G strips and two 2" x 52½" H strips.

**6.** Sew the G strips to opposite sides and H strips to top and bottom of the quilt center; press seams towards the E and F strips.

**7.** Sandwich the batting between the pieced top and a prepared backing piece; baste layers together. Quilt as desired.

**8.** When quilting is complete, remove basting, and trim batting and backing fabric even with raw edges of the pieced top.

**9.** Prepare binding and stitch to quilt front edges, matching raw edges, mitering corners and overlapping ends. Fold binding to back side and stitch in place to finish. ●

*"I love old quilts and reproduction fabrics. I thought it would be cool to use a modern ruler to make a reproduction design."*
*—Holly Daniels*

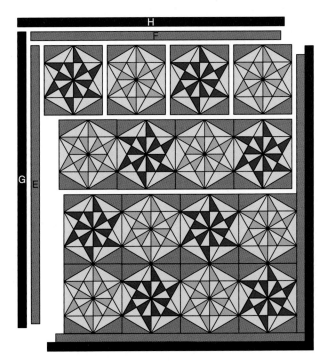

**Patriotic Pinwheels**
Assembly Diagram 52" x 60"

# Stitching a Set-In or Y-Seam

*Many designs using diamonds require set-in or Y-seams. Here are the secrets to success for machine stitching these seams.*

**1.** *Using a pencil, accurately mark dots on seam allowance intersections at the corners and tips of the pieces (Figure A).*

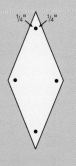

**Figure A**

**2.** *Join two diamond pieces, stopping and starting stitching at the dots; secure seams at dots (Figure B). Press seam open.*

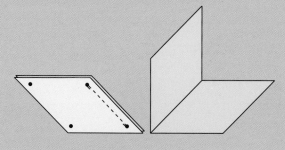

**Figure B**

**3.** *Pin the triangle or square piece to the stitched diamond units, matching the dots (Figure C).*

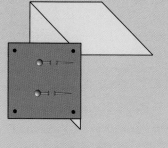

**Figure C**

**4.** *Holding the adjacent seam allowance out of the way, insert the needle into the inner dot, and sew from the inner dot to the outer edge (Figure D).*

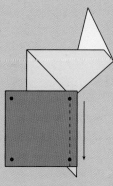

**Figure D**

**5.** *Repeat stitching from the inner dot to the outer edge on the other part of the Y, holding adjacent seam out of the way (Figure E).*

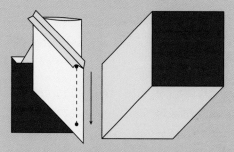

**Figure E**

**6.** *Press seams referring to Figure F.*

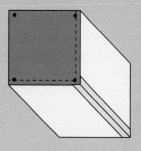

**Figure F**

# Buy Low, Sell High

Design by Gina Gempesaw
Quilted by Carole Whaling

Pick a color palette of light and dark fabrics, piece the easy blocks, and then it's time to play. Arrange the blocks to create the highs and lows.

## Skill Level
Confident Beginner

## Finished Size
Quilt Size: 46" x 60"
Block Size: 5" x 8⅝"
Number of Blocks: 63

## Materials
- ⅝ yard navy tonal
- 1½ yards white solid
- 1⅝ yards gray tonal
- 2¾ yards total assorted blue and green tonals
- Backing to size
- Batting to size
- Thread
- 120-Degree Triangle ruler by EZ Quilting
- Basic sewing tools and supplies

## Project Notes
Read all instructions before beginning this project.

Stitch right sides together using a ¼" seam allowance unless otherwise specified.

Refer to a favorite quilting guide for specific techniques.

Materials and cutting lists assume 40" of usable fabric width.

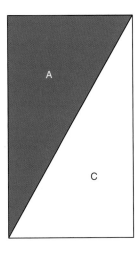

**Light Low-High**
5" x 8⅝" Finished Block
Make 13

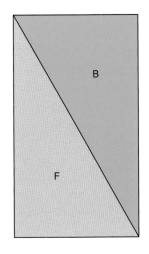

**Dark Low-High**
5" x 8⅝" Finished Block
Make 17

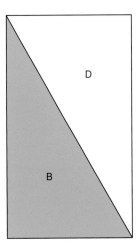

**Reverse Light Low-High**
5" x 8⅝" Finished Block
Make 18

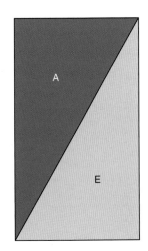

**Reverse Dark Low-High**
5" x 8⅝" Finished Block
Make 15

## Cutting

Refer to Cutting Triangles and General Instructions for 120-Degree Triangle ruler on page 6 for specific cutting instructions.

### From navy tonal:

- Cut 6 (2½" by fabric width) binding strips.

### From white solid:

- Cut 8 (5½" by fabric width) strips.
   Subcut strips into 13 C right-side-up triangles.
   Subcut remaining strips into 18 D wrong-side-up triangles.

### From gray tonal:

- Cut 9 (5½" by fabric width) strips.
   Subcut strips into 15 E right-side-up triangles.
   Subcut remaining strips into 17 F wrong-side-up triangles.

### From assorted blue & green tonals:

- Cut 7 (5½" by fabric width) strips or 28 (5½" x 11") rectangles from scraps.
   Subcut strips or rectangles into 28 A right-side-up triangles.
- Cut 9 (5½" by fabric width) strips or 35 (5½" x 11") rectangles from scraps.
   Subcut strips or rectangles into 35 B wrong-side-up triangles.

## Cutting Triangles

### Right-Side-Up Triangles

**1.** Position ruler on right side of fabric strip or rectangle, lining up 5½" mark with bottom edge of fabric (Figure 1).

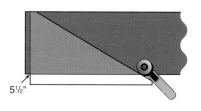

**Figure 1**

**2.** Cut along left short edge and diagonal edge of ruler to cut one triangle right side up, referring again to Figure 1.

**3.** Reverse the ruler, lining up the 5½" mark with fabric top edge and diagonal ruler edge with diagonal fabric edge; cut along right straight edge (Figure 2a). Repeat to cut right-side-up triangles as shown in Figure 2b.

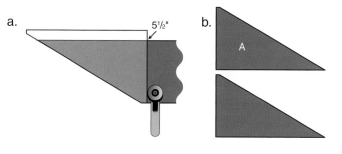

**Figure 2**

## Wrong-Side-Up Triangles

**1.** Position ruler on wrong side of fabric strip or rectangle, lining up 5½" mark with top edge of fabric (Figure 3a).

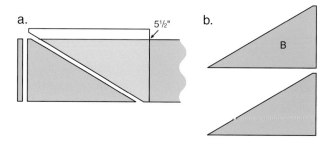

**Figure 3**

**2.** Cut along left short edge and diagonal edge of ruler to cut one triangle wrong side up, referring again to Figure 3a.

**3.** Reverse the ruler, lining up the 5½" mark with fabric top edge and diagonal ruler edge with diagonal fabric edge; cut along right straight edge (Figure 3a). Repeat to cut wrong-side-up triangles as shown in Figure 3b.

## Completing the Quilt Center

**1.** Stitch an A and C triangle together along the long straight edges (Figure 4); press seam toward A. Repeat to make 13 A-C Light Low-High blocks.

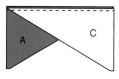

**Figure 4**

**2.** Repeat step 1 to make 17 B-F Dark Low-High blocks, 18 B-D Reverse Light Low-High blocks and 15 A-E Reverse Dark Low-High blocks referring to the block diagams.

**3.** Refer to the Assembly Diagram and arrange blocks into seven rows of nine blocks each as desired to make a zigzag stripe pattern.

**4.** Stitch blocks into rows as arranged; pressing seams in opposite directions row to row.

**5.** Stitch rows together and press seams in one direction or open to reduce bulk.

## Completing the Quilt

**1.** Sandwich the batting between the pieced top and a prepared backing piece; baste layers together. Quilt as desired.

**2.** When quilting is complete, remove basting, and trim batting and backing fabric even with raw edges of the pieced top.

**3.** Prepare binding and stitch to quilt front edges, matching raw edges, mitering corners and overlapping ends. Fold binding to back side and stitch in place to finish. ●

*"The ups and downs of the stock market inspired the direction of the triangles in this quilt!" —Gina Gempesaw*

**Buy Low, Sell High**
Alternate Queen Size
Assembly Diagram 80" x 95"
Make 176 blocks and lay out into 11 rows
of 16 blocks each to increase quilt to queen size.

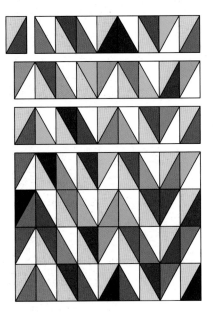

**Buy Low, Sell High**
Assembly Diagram 45" x 60"

# Boomerang

**Designed & Quilted by Julie Weaver**

This lovely bed runner would look terrific in any color, and using the 120-Degree Triangle ruler makes the process stress free.

## Skill Level
Intermediate

## Finished Size
Runner Size: Approximately 53½" x 18"
Block Sizes: 6½" x 5½" and 3" x 5½"
Number of Blocks: 26 and 4

## Materials
- ¼ yard navy print
- ¼ yard white solid
- ½ yard navy dot
- ½ yard green dot
- ⅝ yard navy/white print
- ¾ yard green print
- Backing to size
- Batting to size
- Thread
- 120-Degree Triangle ruler by EZ Quilting
- Basic sewing tools and supplies

## Project Notes
Read all instructions before beginning this project.

Stitch right sides together using a ¼" seam allowance unless otherwise specified.

Refer to a favorite quilting guide for specific techniques.

Materials and cutting lists assume 40" of usable fabric width.

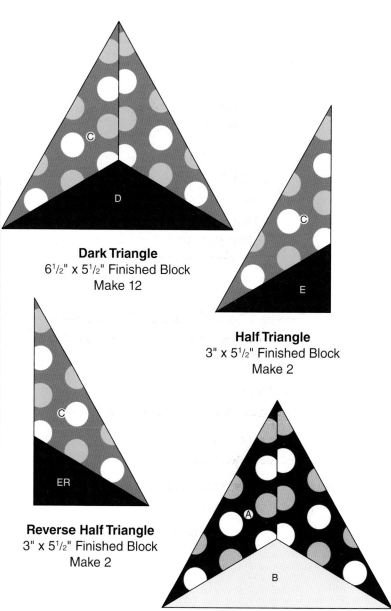

**Dark Triangle**
6½" x 5½" Finished Block
Make 12

**Half Triangle**
3" x 5½" Finished Block
Make 2

**Reverse Half Triangle**
3" x 5½" Finished Block
Make 2

**Light Triangle**
6½" x 5½" Finished Block
Make 14

## Cutting

Refer to General Instructions for 120-Degree Triangle ruler on page 6 for specific cutting instructions.

### From navy print:

- Cut 2 (2½" by fabric width) strips.
  Subcut strips into 12 D full triangles.
- Cut 2 E half triangles and 2 reverse ER half triangles from remaining fabric.

### From white solid:

- Cut 2 (2½" by fabric width) strips.
  Subcut strips into 14 B full triangles.

### From navy dot:

- Cut 4 (2½" by fabric width) strips.
  Subcut strips into 28 A full triangles.

### From green dot:

- Cut 4 (2½" by fabric width) strips.
  Subcut strips into 24 C full triangles.
- Cut 4 C full triangles from remaining fabric.

### From navy/white print:

- Cut 4 (3" by fabric width) H/I strips.

### From green print:

- Cut 3 (1½" by fabric width) F/G strips.
- Cut 5 (2½" by fabric width) binding strips.

> ## Designer's Tip
>
> *The triangles used in this runner are made from 2½" strips of fabric. By following the general instructions for this ruler, you should get eight full triangles from one 2½" by fabric width strip.*

## Completing the Blocks

**1.** Mark ¼" from the points of all triangles. Stitch two A triangles together starting and stopping ¼" from the points as shown in Figure 1 to make 14 A units. Press seam to one side.

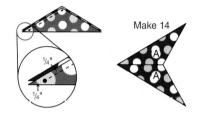

**Figure 1**

**2.** Stitch a B triangle to an A unit referring to Stitching a Set-In or Y-Seam on page 27 to complete a Light Triangle block as shown in the block diagram.

**3.** Repeat steps 1 and 2 to make 14 Light Triangle blocks.

**4.** Repeat steps 1 and 2 with C and D triangles to make 12 Dark Triangle blocks referring to the block diagram.

**5.** Stitch an E triangle to one short side of a C triangle to make a Half Triangle block (Figure 2). Repeat to make two half blocks.

**Figure 2**

**6.** Stitch an ER triangle on the opposite short side of each remaining C triangle to make two Reverse Half Triangle blocks referring to the block diagram.

## Completing Quilt Center

**1.** Arrange the Light, Dark and Half Triangle blocks as shown in Figure 3 to make the top and bottom rows of quilt center.

Top Row

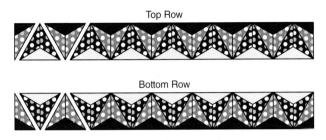

Bottom Row

**Figure 3**

**2.** Stitch blocks together as arranged. Press seams toward Dark Triangle blocks.

**3.** Stitch rows together with Light Triangle block bases matching. Press seam open.

**4.** Stitch F/G strips together to make one long strip; press seams open or to one side.

**5.** Measure quilt center to determine border lengths referring to Determining Border Lengths on page 78. Cut two each F top and bottom borders and G side borders using measurements determined.

**6.** Stitch F to top and bottom, and G to sides of quilt center. Press seams toward borders.

**7.** Repeat steps 4–6 with H/I strips to add second borders.

### Designer's Tip

*I was pleasantly surprised at how easy the blocks were to make! Starting and stopping sewing ¼" from each end is a definite "must-do." This really does make it easier to construct the triangular blocks. Conscientious pressing will also make assembly much easier!*

## Completing the Quilt

**1.** Sandwich the batting between the pieced top and a prepared backing piece; baste layers together. Quilt as desired.

**2.** When quilting is complete, remove basting, and trim batting and backing fabric even with raw edges of the pieced top.

**3.** Prepare binding and stitch to quilt front edges, matching raw edges, mitering corners and overlapping ends. Fold binding to back side and stitch in place to finish. ●

*"The 'ruler challenge' was the inspiration for this runner! I am not a 'ruler' or a 'gadget' girl. I've got about three or four rulers I use regularly and do not generally buy any specialty rulers, so this project definitely was a challenge for me. I discovered it's sort of fun to try something new and out of my comfort zone!" —Julie Weaver*

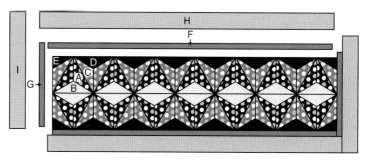

**Boomerang**
Assembly Diagram 53¹⁄₂" x 18"

# Stars at Night Are Big & Bright

Designed & Quilted by Chris Malone

Create a stunning bed runner for your bed no matter what size it is. This pattern makes it easy to add or subtract length, and the blocks are easier than they look.

## Skill Level

Intermediate

## Finished Size

Bed Runner Size: 105" x 17½"
Block Size: 15" side to side
Number of Blocks: 7

## Materials

- 1 yard each gold and red prints
- 1½ yard black print
- Backing to size
- Batting to size
- Thread
- 7 (1⅛"-diameter) cover buttons
- 120-Degree Triangle ruler by EZ Quilting
- Basic sewing tools and supplies

## Project Notes

Read all instructions before beginning this project.

Stitch right sides together using a ¼" seam allowance unless otherwise specified.

Refer to a favorite quilting guide for specific techniques.

Materials and cutting lists assume 40" of usable fabric width.

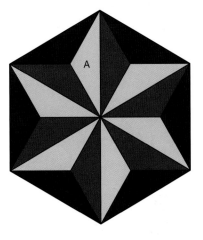

**Star**
15" Side to Side
Make 7

## Cutting

Refer to General Instructions for 120-Degree Triangle ruler on page 6 for specific cutting instructions.

## From each gold and red print:

- Cut 9 (3" by fabric width) strips
  Subcut strips into 42 A triangles with 3" dashed line of ruler aligned with folded edge of fabric.

## From black print:

- Cut 9 (3" by fabric width) strips.
  Subcut strips into 42 A triangles with 3" dashed line of ruler aligned with folded edge of fabric.
- Cut 7 (2¼" by fabric width) binding strips.
- Cut 1 (2½" by fabric width) strip.
  Subcut strips into 7 (2¼"-diameter) circles for cover buttons.

### Designer's Tip

*Spray starch is really helpful when sewing with bias edges. Spray on fabric and press before cutting for the truest cuts, and the edges will be less likely to stretch.*

### Completing the Blocks

**1.** Following the color placement and orientation as shown in Figure 1 and referring to Stitching a Set-In or Y-Seam on page 27, sew one each red, gold and black A triangles together using a set-in seam to assemble a wedge; press. Repeat to make 42 wedges.

Make 42

**Figure 1**

**2.** Sew three wedges together to form a half-block as shown in Figure 2; press. Repeat to make a second half-block.

Make 2

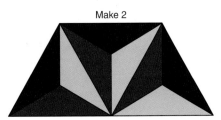

**Figure 2**

**3.** Sew two half-blocks together to make a block referring to the block diagram; press.

**4.** Repeat steps 2 and 3 to make a total of 7 blocks.

### Completing the Runner

**1.** Referring to Assembly Diagram for orientation, sew blocks together to form bed runner.

**2.** Sandwich the batting between the pieced top and a prepared backing piece; baste layers together. Quilt as desired.

**3.** When quilting is complete, remove basting, and trim batting and backing fabric even with raw edges of the pieced top.

**4.** Prepare binding and stitch to quilt front as shown in Binding Inside Corners on page 41, matching raw edges, mitering corners and overlapping ends. Fold binding to back side and stitch in place to finish.

**5.** Following manufacturer's directions, cover buttons with black print circles and sew in place in the center of each star block. ●

*"These stars go together easily since cutting with the 120-Degree Triangle ruler is so accurate." —Chris Malone*

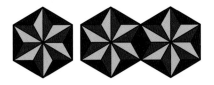

**Stars at Night Are Big & Bright Table Runner**
Alternate Assembly Diagram 45" x 17½"
Make 3 blocks for table runner.

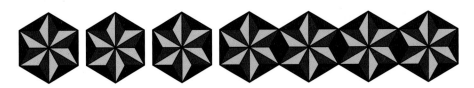

**Stars at Night Are Big & Bright Bed Runner**
Assembly Diagram 105" x 17½"

# Binding Inside Corners

Use either bias or straight single-fold binding to bind projects with inside corners. Single-fold binding helps decrease the bulk of the seams in those corners where blocks join. Single-fold bias binding stretches to accommodate the stretch on the inside corner. The following method also works with a double-layered binding.

**1.** To make single-fold binding, cut 1¾"-wide strips from the binding fabric. Join the strips on the short ends to make an appropriate length strip.

**2.** Fold ¼" to the wrong side on one long edge and press to hold.

**3.** Staystitch close to the ¼" seam allowance through the layers of your project at each inside corner as shown in Figure A.

1/4"

**Figure A**

**4.** Clip into the corner almost to the seam allowance as shown in Figure B.

**Figure B**

**5.** Leaving a 12" tail, match the raw edge of the binding to the raw edge of the project top and stitch using a ¼" seam allowance, mitering at the outer corners.

**6.** Sew the binding to the edge of each inside corner, leaving the needle down at the clip as shown in Figure C.

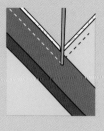

**Figure C**

**7.** Turn the project top and sew along the adjacent side of the inside corner.

**8.** Continue sewing binding all around, overlapping at the beginning and end.

**9.** Clip into each inside corner of binding just to the stitching line referring to Figure D.

**Figure D**

**10.** To sew the binding down at the inside corners, referring to Figure E, fold down the left side and then the right side, and hand-stitch the miter that forms. Turn to the back side and repeat to complete the binding.

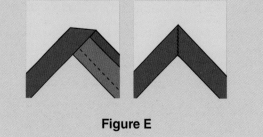

**Figure E**

# Marching Diamonds

Designed & Quilted by Chris Malone

Cutting accurate diamonds is so easy with the proper ruler, and framing each diamond with simple strips really emphasizes the interesting shape.

## Skill Level
Beginner

## Finished Size
Quilt Size: 48" x 47½"

Block Size: 7" x 17"

Number of Blocks: 33

## Materials
- ⅝ yard green/blue dot
- 1 yard aqua print
- 1½ yard light gray dot
- 1⅞ yard white tonal
- Backing to size
- Batting to size
- Thread
- 45-Degree Diamond ruler by EZ Quilting
- Basic sewing tools and supplies

## Project Notes
Read all instructions before beginning this project.

Stitch right sides together using a ¼" seam allowance unless otherwise specified.

Refer to a favorite quilting guide for specific techniques.

Materials and cutting lists assume 40" of usable fabric width.

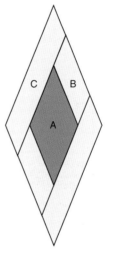

**Light Framed Diamond**
7" x 17" Finished Block
Make 12

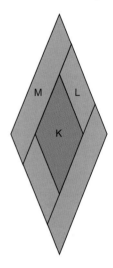

**Dark Framed Diamond**
7" x 17" Finished Block
Make 21

## Cutting
Refer to General Instructions for 45-Degree Diamond ruler on page 5 for specific cutting instructions.

### From green/blue dot:
- Cut 4 (4" by fabric width) strips.
  Subcut strips into 20 A diamonds. Set aside eight of the A diamonds for setting blocks.

### From aqua print:
- Cut 4 (4" by fabric width) strips.
  Subcut strips into 21 K diamonds.
- Cut 5 (2¼" by fabric width) binding strips.

## From light gray dot:
- Cut 23 (2" by fabric width) strips.
  Subcut strips into 42 each 2" x 8½" L and 2" x 12½" M rectangles.

## From white tonal:
- Cut 1 (3" by fabric width) strip.
  Subcut strip into 4 (3" x 8") J rectangles.
- Cut 23 (2" by fabric width) strips.
  Subcut 13 strips into 24 each 2" x 8½" B and 2" x 12½" C rectangles.
  Subcut 3 strips into 12 (2" x 7") E rectangles.
  Subcut 4 strips into 12 (2" x 12") F rectangles.
  Subcut 1 strip into 4 (2" x 10") H rectangles.
  Subcut 2 strips into 4 (2" x 12") I rectangles.

## Completing the Blocks

**1.** Match a B long edge to the top edge of an A diamond, offsetting the straight short ends by ¼" and 2" referring to Figure 1; stitch in place.

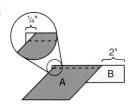

**Figure 1**

**Designer's Tip**

*Spray starch (or starch alternative) is really helpful when sewing with bias edges. Spray pieces and iron before cutting, for edges less likely to stretch and for the truest cuts.*

**2.** Repeat on opposite side of diamond as shown in Figure 2. Press seams open.

**Figure 2**

**3.** Trim ends of B strips to match A diamond edges (Figure 3). **Note:** *Always sew the strips in the same order and positions on each diamond.*

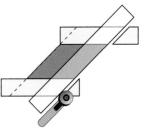

**Figure 3**

**4.** Repeat steps 1–3 with C strips to complete one Light Framed Diamond block (Figure 4).

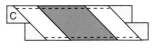

**Figure 4**

**5.** Repeat steps 1–4 to make a total of 12 Light Framed Diamond blocks.

**6.** Repeat steps 1–5 with K diamonds and L and M strips to complete 21 Dark Framed Diamond blocks.

## Completing the Side Setting Triangles

**1.** Cut six of remaining eight A diamonds in half horizontally to make 12 D triangles and two vertically to make four G triangles (Figure 5).

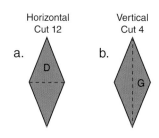

**Figure 5**

**2.** Stitch an E strip to the right-hand long edge of a D triangle, offsetting E as done in step 1 of Completing the Blocks; press seam open and trim (Figure 6a).

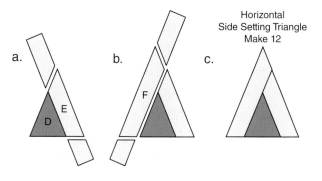

**Figure 6**

**3.** Repeat with F on opposite D edge to complete 12 horizontal side setting triangles referring to Figure 6b and c.

**4.** Repeat steps 2 and 3 with G triangles and H and I strips referring to Figure 7 a–c to complete four vertical side setting triangles.

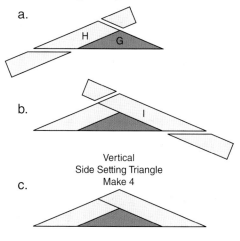

**Figure 7**

## Completing the Quilt

**1.** Arrange the diamond blocks, horizontal and vertical side setting triangles and J rectangles into nine diagonal rows referring to Figure 8.

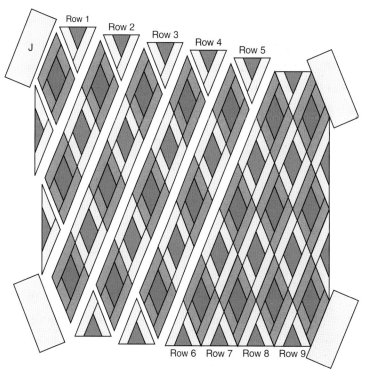

**Figure 8**

**2.** Stitch units together in rows, offsetting the tips ¼" (Figure 9). Press seams open.

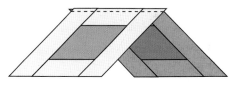

**Figure 9**

**3.** Stitch diagonal rows together referring to Matching Angled Seams on page 47; press seams open. ***Note:*** *The quilt's outer edges will be uneven.*

**4.** To trim top and bottom edges of quilt top, line up a long straightedge ruler 3" from D tip of side setting triangles referring to Figure 10. Trim, sliding the ruler as needed. Repeat on side edges, placing edge of ruler 3" from tip of vertical side setting triangles as shown in Figure 11.

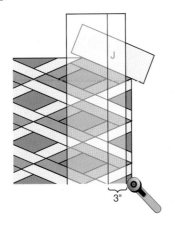

**Figure 10**

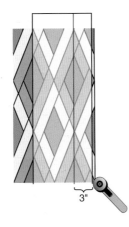

**Figure 11**

**5.** To stabilize the bias edges on all sides, staystitch all around the quilt top, ³⁄₁₆" from the edge.

**6.** Sandwich the batting between the pieced top and a prepared backing piece; baste layers together. Quilt as desired.

**7.** When quilting is complete, remove basting, and trim batting and backing fabric even with raw edges of the pieced top.

**8.** Prepare binding and stitch to quilt front edges, matching raw edges, mitering corners and overlapping ends. Fold binding to back side and stitch in place to finish. ●

*"Contemporary baby quilts do not necessarily have to be traditional baby motifs in pastel shades. Today's baby quilts often feature simple shapes in clean, fresh palettes." —Chris Malone*

**Marching Diamonds**
Placement Diagram 48" x 47¹⁄₂"

# Matching Angled Seams

To make sure your angled seams match well between blocks, units or rows:

• Press seams in opposite directions as you would if matching straight seams that are to be butted or nested together (Photo A).

**Photo A**

• Position a pin ¼" from the edge through the seams at the intersection of the seam allowances where the seams will cross to form an X. Pin the edges together (Photo B).

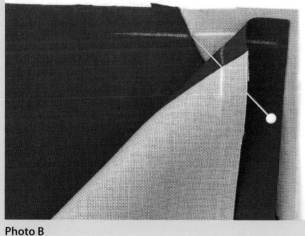

**Photo B**

• Stitch the joining seam, removing the pins as you come to them. Do not stitch over pins (Photo C).

**Photo C**

• Press the joining seam open to distribute fabric bulk (Photo D).

**Photo D**

# Dripping With Diamonds

Design by Nancy Scott
Quilted by Masterpiece Quilting

This quilt is surprisingly quick to make with the help of a 45-Degree Diamond ruler. It looks much more difficult than it is.

## Skill Level
Confident Beginner

## Finished Size
Quilt Size: 48" x 74½"

## Materials
- ⅜ yard each 6 bright batiks
- ⅝ yard purple batik
- 3⅜ yards light green batik
- Backing to size
- Batting to size
- Thread
- 45-Degree Diamond ruler by E-Z Quilter
- Basic sewing tools and supplies

## Project Notes
Read all instructions before beginning this project.

Stitch right sides together using a ¼" seam allowance unless otherwise specified.

Refer to a favorite quilting guide for specific techniques.

Materials and cutting lists assume 40" of usable fabric width.

## Cutting
Refer to General Instructions for 45-Degree Diamond ruler on page 5 for specific cutting instructions.

### From each bright batik:
- Cut 2 (4" by fabric width) strips.
  Subcut strips into 7 A diamonds of each color.

### From purple batik:
- Cut 7 (2½" by fabric width) binding strips.

### From light green batik:
- Cut 9 (4" by fabric width) strips.
  Subcut strips into 60 B diamonds.
- Trim remaining yardage to 75" by fabric width.
  Subcut lengthwise into 4 (4½" x 75") C strips
  and 2 (7½" x 75") D strips.
  Cut remainder into 2 (4" x 75") strips; subcut into
  26 B diamonds for a total of 86 B diamonds.

## Completing the Vertical Rows
**1.** Arrange A diamonds in vertical rows referring to Assembly Diagram.

**2.** Stitch B diamonds onto opposite sides of A diamonds (Figure 1) Press seams toward A triangles.

**Figure 1**

**3.** Stitch B-A-B units together matching A diamond tips to form vertical rows (Figure 2); press.

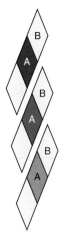

**Figure 2**

**4.** Stitch a B diamond on each top and bottom A diamond on three of the rows.

**5.** Square up and trim sides, top and bottom of rows to measure 4" x 75", making sure to leave ¼" on each side of A diamonds for seam allowance, referring to Figure 3 to make three vertical 8-Diamond Rows.

8-Diamond Row
Make 3

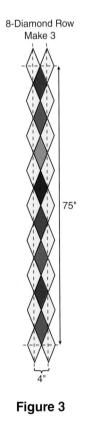

75"

4"

**Figure 3**

**6.** Add another B-A-B unit to two remaining vertical rows. Repeat step 5 trimming rows to 4" x 75" completing two 9-Diamond Rows referring to Figure 4 and the Assembly Diagram for color placement.

9-Diamond Row
Make 2

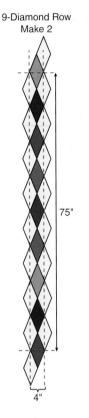

75"

4"

**Figure 4**

**7.** Refer to the Assembly Diagram and stitch the diamond vertical rows and C and D strips together to complete quilt center.

> ## Designer's Tip
>
> *When working with biased edges on the diamonds, be sure not to over-handle the edges while pressing or sewing; it can cause them to stretch out of shape.*

## Completing the Quilt

**1.** Sandwich the batting between the pieced top and a prepared backing piece; baste layers together. Quilt as desired.

**2.** When quilting is complete, remove basting, and trim batting and backing fabric even with raw edges of the pieced top.

**3.** Prepare binding and stitch to quilt front edges, matching raw edges, mitering corners and overlapping ends. Fold binding to back side and stitch in place to finish. ●

*"I have always liked diamonds (what girl doesn't?), and this quilt does a great job of showcasing them."* —Nancy Scott

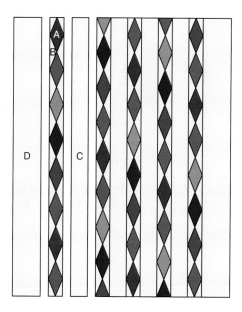

**Dripping With Diamonds**
Assembly Diagram 48" x 74½"

# LeMoyne Star

Design by Nancy Scott
Quilted by Masterpiece Quilting

Here's a LeMoyne Star block with a twist. This classic is made with the 45-Degree Diamond ruler and is destined to be a favorite.

## Skill Level
Confident Beginner

## Finished Size
Quilt Size: 82" x 82"
Block Size: 9½" x 9½"
Number of Blocks: 25

## Materials
- 3⅜ yards black tonal
- 4¼ yards white solid
- Backing to size
- Batting to size
- Thread
- 45-Degree Diamond ruler by EZ Quilting
- Basic sewing tools and supplies

## Project Notes
Read all instructions before beginning this project.

Stitch right sides together using a ¼" seam allowance unless otherwise specified.

Refer to a favorite quilting guide for specific techniques.

Materials and cutting lists assume 40" of usable fabric width.

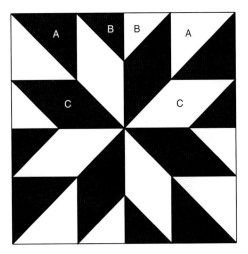

**LeMoyne Star**
9½" x 9½" Finished Block
Make 25

## Cutting
Refer to General Instructions for 45-Degree Diamond ruler on page 5 for specific cutting instructions.

## From black tonal:
- Cut 1 (85" by fabric width) strip.
    Subcut strip lengthwise into 4 (2½" x 85") binding strips, 2 (5½" x 82") I strips and 2 (5½" x 72") J strips.
    Subcut remainder of strip into 4 (2½" x 85") strips and cut strips into C diamonds.
- Cut 1 (2½" by fabric width) strip.
    Subcut strip into C diamonds to make a total of 100 black C diamonds.

- Cut 5 (3⅝" by fabric width) strips.
  Subcut strips into 50 (3⅝") squares.
  Cut each square on 1 diagonal to make
  100 black A triangles.
- Cut 4 (2⅞" by fabric width) strips.
  Subcut strips into 50 (2⅞") squares. Cut each
  square on 1 diagonal to make 100 black
  B triangles.

### From white solid:
- Cut 1 (72" by fabric width) strip.
  Subcut strip lengthwise into 2 (2½" x 72")
  G borders, 2 (2½" x 68") H borders.
  Subcut remainder of strip lengthwise into
  3 (10" x 72") strips. Cut strips into 16 (10")
  D squares. Cut remainder of strip into
  4 (2½" x 52") strips; subcut strips into
  C diamonds.
- Cut 4 (2½" by fabric width) strips.
  Subcut strips into C diamonds to make a total
  of 100 white C diamonds.

- Cut 5 (3⅝" by fabric width) strips.
  Subcut strips into 50 (3⅝") squares.
  Cut each square on 1 diagonal to make
  100 white A triangles.
- Cut 4 (2⅞" by fabric width) strips.
  Subcut strips into 50 (2⅞") squares.
  Cut each square on 1 diagonal to make
  100 white B triangles.
- Cut 2 (14⅝" by fabric width) strips.
  Subcut strips into 4 (14⅝") squares.
  Cut each square on both diagonals to
  make 16 E triangles.
  From reminder of strip, cut 2 (7⅝") squares;
  cut each square on 1 diagonal to make
  4 F triangles.

## Designer's Tip

*While it's tempting to round the ⅝" and ⅞" cutting measurements up to ¾" and a whole number, that ⅛" does make a difference for accurate piecing.*

## Completing the Blocks

**1.** Stitch a black B to a white C angled side referring to Figure 1; press seam toward B. Repeat to make 100 B-C units in this color combination and 100 units in the opposite color combination referring again to Figure 1.

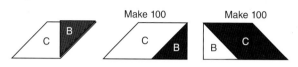

Make 100          Make 100

**Figure 1**

**2.** Refer to Figure 2 to stitch A triangles to the B-C units making 100 of each color combination. Press seams toward black pieces.

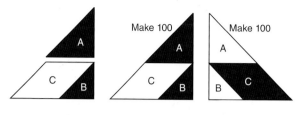

Make 100          Make 100

**Figure 2**

**3.** Stitch A-B-C units together referring to Figure 3 to make 100 quarter-blocks.

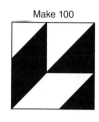

Make 100

**Figure 3**

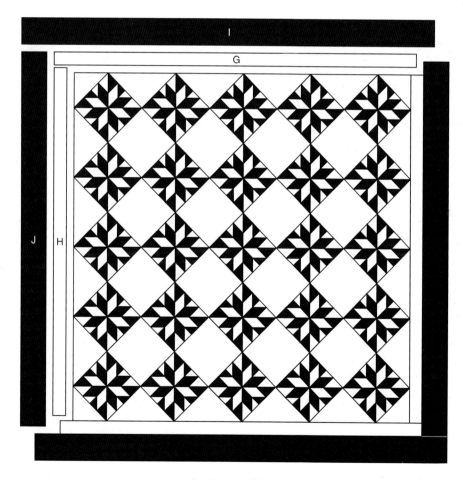

**LeMoyne Star**
Assembly Diagram 82" x 82"

**4.** Refer to the block diagram to stitch quarter-blocks together to form half-block rows and then full blocks. Press seams in opposition directions between rows and refer to Spinning Centers to Reduce Bulk on page 17 to press block center. Repeat to make 25 blocks.

## Completing the Quilt Center

**1.** Arrange LeMoyne Star blocks, D squares, and F and E setting triangles in nine diagonal rows as shown in Figure 4.

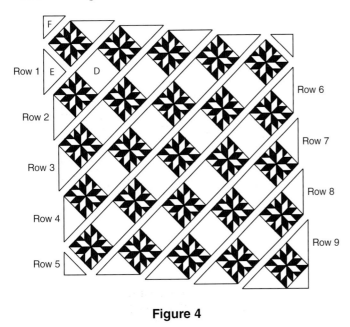

**Figure 4**

**2.** Stitch rows together as arranged matching seams; press seams in opposite directions in adjacent rows.

**3.** Stitch H borders to quilt center sides and G borders to top and bottom of quilt center referring to the Assembly Diagram.

**4.** Stitch J borders to quilt center sides and I borders to top and bottom of quilt center referring again to the Assembly Diagram.

**5.** Sandwich the batting between the pieced top and a prepared backing piece; baste layers together. Quilt as desired.

**6.** When quilting is complete, remove basting, and trim batting and backing fabric even with raw edges of the pieced top.

**7.** Prepare binding and stitch to quilt front edges, matching raw edges, mitering corners and overlapping ends. Fold binding to back side and stitch in place to finish. ●

*"I love old quilts and the vintage block patterns. We have an antique quilt that my great-great-grandmother pieced by hand, and it is a LeMoyne Star." —Nancy Scott*

**LeMoyne Star**
Alternate Size Option
Assembly Diagram 46" x 59"
For lap-size quilt, make 12 blocks, 10 F side setting triangles and 4 E corner triangles.
Cut H/G border strips 1½" wide and J/I border strips 3" wide by appropriate lengths.

# Lilies of the Field

Designed & Quilted by Julie Weaver

Turn 45-Degree Diamonds into beautiful flowers with the help of a bit of fusible appliqué and the use of a couple of rulers.

## Skill Level

Intermediate

## Finished Size

Runner Size: 72" x 29"
Block Size: 9½" x 9½"
Number of Blocks: 14

## Materials

- ¾ yard rose print 1
- ¾ yard green print
- 1⅛ yards cream print
- 1⅛ yards rose print 2
- ½ yard fusible web
- Backing to size
- Batting to size
- Thread
- 45-Degree Diamond ruler by EZ Quilting®
- Flying Geese ruler by EZ Quilting®
- Basic sewing tools and supplies

## Project Notes

Read all instructions before beginning this project.

Stitch right sides together using a ¼" seam allowance unless otherwise specified.

Refer to a favorite quilting guide for specific techniques.

Materials and cutting lists assume 40" of usable fabric width.

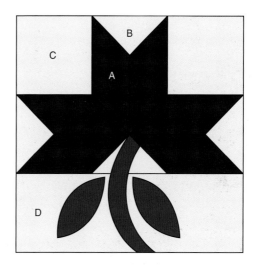

**Lilies of the Field**
9¹/₂" x 9¹/₂" Finished Block
Make 14

## Cutting

Refer to General Instructions for 45-Degree Diamond and Flying Geese rulers on page 3 for specific cutting instructions.

### From rose print 1:

- Cut 9 (2½" by fabric width) strips.
  Subcut strips into 84 A diamonds aligning the 2½" line on ruler with long edge of fabric.

### From green print:

- Cut 5 (2" by fabric width) E/F strips.
- Cut appliqué pieces as per patterns.

## From cream print:
- Cut 5 (2½" by fabric width) strips.
  Subcut strips into 56 B triangles with Flying Geese ruler aligning the 2½" line of Side A with long edge of fabric.
- Cut 7 (3¼" by fabric width) strips.
  Subcut strips into 28 (3¼") C squares and 14 (3¼" x 10") D rectangles.

## From rose print 2:
- Cut 2 (1¾" by fabric width) strips.
  Subcut strips into 2 (1¾" x 22½") G strips.
- Cut 4 (4" by fabric width) H strips.
- Cut 6 (2½" by fabric width) binding strips.

## Completing the Blocks

**1.** To make one block, select six A diamonds, four B triangles, two each C squares and leaves, and one each D rectangle and stem.

**2.** Referring to Figure 1 and Stitching a Set-In or Y-Seam on page 27, sew two A diamonds and one B triangle together. Repeat to make three A-B units.

Make 3

**Figure 1**

**Designer's Tip**

*While sewing the set-in seams, accurate ¼" seams and conscientious pressing helps make assembly easier.*

**2.** Sew three A-B units together along with one B triangle as shown in Figure 2 to complete a flower unit.

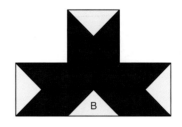

**Figure 2**

**3.** Sew two C squares on opposite sides of the flower unit as shown in Figure 3.

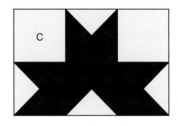

**Figure 3**

**4.** Sew a D rectangle onto the bottom of the flower unit as shown in Figure 4.

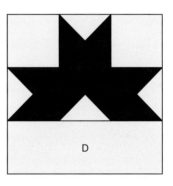

**Figure 4**

**5.** Referring to Raw-Edge Fusible Appliqué Instructions on page 61 and the block drawing; prepare and fuse two leaf and one stem appliqués in place. Machine- or hand-appliqué in place.

**6.** Repeat steps 1–5 to make a total of 14 blocks.

## Completing the Quilt

**1.** Referring to the Assembly Diagram, arrange and sew seven blocks together to form a row; press seams in one direction. Repeat to make a second row; press seams in opposite direction from first row.

**2.** Sew rows together to complete the quilt center; press.

**3.** Join the E/F strips on the short ends to make a long strip; press. Subcut strip into two (2" x 19½") E strips and two (2" x 70") F strips.

**4.** Sew the E strips to opposite sides and F strips to top and bottom of the quilt center. Press seams toward the strips.

**5.** Join H strips on short ends to make a long strip; press. Subcut strip into two (4" x 72½") H strips.

**6.** Sew the G strips to opposite sides and H strips to the top and bottom of the quilt center to complete the quilt top. Press seams toward the G and H strips.

**7.** Sandwich the batting between the pieced top and a prepared backing piece; baste layers together. Quilt as desired.

**8.** When quilting is complete, remove basting, and trim batting and backing fabric even with raw edges of the pieced top.

**9.** Prepare binding and stitch to quilt front edges, matching raw edges, mitering corners and overlapping ends. Fold binding to back side and stitch in place to finish. ●

*"Fusing the stems and leaves of the pieced flowers onto the block after the block is sewn allows for a little wiggle room in covering up any points that don't match exactly."* —Julie Weaver

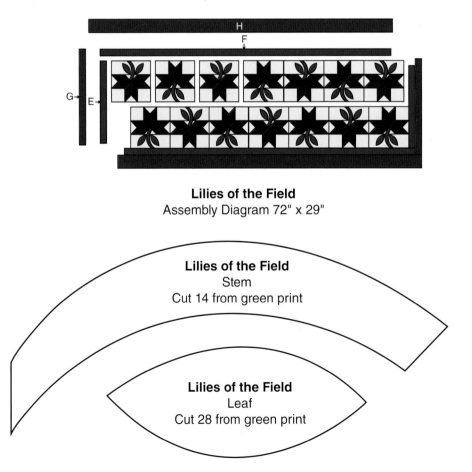

**Lilies of the Field**
Assembly Diagram 72" x 29"

**Lilies of the Field**
Stem
Cut 14 from green print

**Lilies of the Field**
Leaf
Cut 28 from green print

# Raw-Edge Fusible Appliqué

One of the easiest ways to appliqué is the fusible-web method. Paper-backed fusible web motifs are fused to the wrong side of fabric, cut out and then fused to a foundation fabric and stitched in place by hand or machine. You can use this method for raw- or turned-edge appliqué.

**1.** If the appliqué motif is directional, it should be reversed for raw-edge fusible appliqué. If doing several identical appliqué motifs, trace reverse motif shapes onto template material to make reusable templates.

**2.** Use templates or trace the appliqué motif shapes onto paper side of paper-backed fusible web. Leave at least ½" between shapes. Cut out shapes leaving a margin around traced lines.

**3.** Follow manufacturer's instructions and fuse shapes to wrong side of fabric as indicated on pattern for color and number to cut.

**4.** Cut out appliqué shapes on traced lines and remove paper backing from fusible web. **Note:** If doing turned-edge appliqué, cut out appliqué ⅛" outside the traced lines. Then fold edges to wrong side on traced lines.

**5.** Again following manufacturer's instructions, arrange and fuse pieces on the foundation fabric referring to appliqué motif included in pattern.

**6.** Hand- or machine-stitch around edges. **Note:** Position a light- to mediumweight stabilizer behind the appliqué motif to keep the fabric from puckering during machine stitching. Some stitch possibilities include machine- or hand-satin or zigzag, buttonhole or blanket and running stitch.

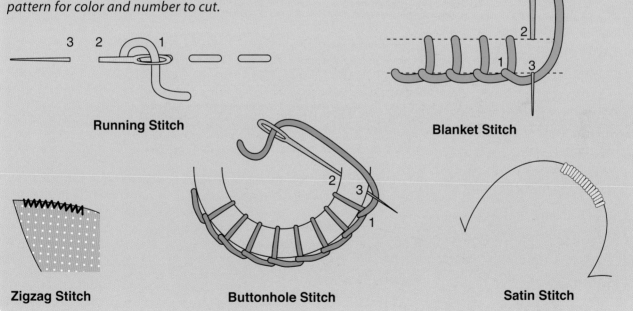

Running Stitch

Blanket Stitch

Zigzag Stitch

Buttonhole Stitch

Satin Stitch

# Ornamental Arches

Designed & Quilted by Amy Krasnansky

Make Drunkard's Path blocks in an unconventional way
using a Double Wedding Ring Single Arc ruler.

## Skill Level
Intermediate

## Finished Size
Quilt Size: 72" x 87"
Block Size: 7½" x 7½"
Number of Blocks: 80

## Materials

- 48 (10") precut squares or scraps (at least
  10" square) assorted blue, green and purple batiks
- 1⅛ yards dark blue
- 2⅔ yards blue/green/purple batik
- 3 yards light gray tonal
- Backing to size
- Batting to size
- Thread
- Freezer paper (optional)
- Temporary fabric glue
- Double Wedding Ring Single Arc ruler
  by EZ Quilting
- Basic sewing tools and supplies

## Project Notes
Read all instructions before beginning this project.

Stitch right sides together using a ¼" seam allowance
unless otherwise specified.

Refer to a favorite quilting guide for specific
techniques.

Materials and cutting lists assume 40" of usable
fabric width.

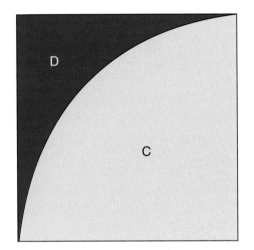

**Large Arch**
7½" x 7½" Finished Block
Make 32

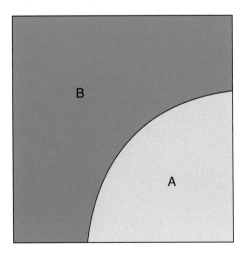

**Small Arch**
7½" x 7½" Finished Block
Make 48

## Cutting

Refer to Cutting Small & Large Perimeter & Corner Pieces and General Instructions for Double Wedding Ring Single Arc ruler on page 7 for specific cutting instructions.

### From assorted batik squares or scraps:

- Cut 12 A small corners, 36 B small perimeters, 12 C large corners and 20 D large perimeters. **Note:** *Combinations of A and B, C and D, and B and D can be cut from a single square; refer to Assembly Diagram for color suggestions.*

### From dark blue:

- Cut 7 (1½" by fabric width) E/F strips.
- Cut 9 (2½" by fabric width) binding strips.

### From blue/green/purple batik:

- Cut 4 (5½" by fabric length) strips.
    Trim strips to 2 each 5½" x 77½" G borders and 5½" x 72½" H borders.

### From light gray tonal:

- Cut 6 (10" by fabric width) strips.
    Subcut strips into 24 (10") squares. Subcut 12 squares into 1 each A small corners and B small perimeters, and the remaining 12 squares into 1 each C large corners and D large perimeters for a total of 12 of each piece.
- Cut 2 (8" by fabric width) strips.
    Subcut strips into 8 (8") squares. Subcut squares into 8 C large corners for a total of 20 light gray large corners.
- Cut 4 (6" by fabric width) strips.
    Subcut strips into 24 (6") squares. Subcut squares into 24 A small corners for a total of 36 light gray A small corners.

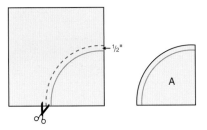

*The intended finished outer border sizes are 5" and 7", but strips can be cut up to 6" and 8" wide and slightly longer to ensure that the quilt can be squared up and trimmed.*

## Cutting Small & Large Perimeter & Corner Pieces

**Designer's Tip**

*You can cut both an A and B together or C and D together from a 9" or 10" square. You can also fit both a B and D in opposite corners of a 10" square.*

### Cutting A Small Corners

**1.** Position the ruler on the wrong side of a scrap or across the corner of a 10" square, leaving a ¼" seam allowance on each side of the straight edges (Figure 1).

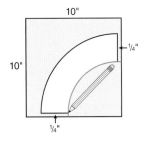

**Figure 1**

**Designer's Tip**

*Using a small-radius rotary cutter or short, sharp shears instead of standard fabric shears to cut the curved edges makes cutting easier.*

**2.** Draw along the smaller arc of the ruler. **Do not cut on this line.** Cut approximately ½" outside the drawn arc referring to Figure 2.

**Figure 2**

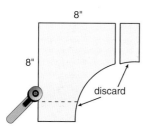

**3.** If using 10" squares, trim the square to 8" as shown in Figure 3 and then follow Instructions in Cutting B Small Perimeters.

**Figure 3**

## Cutting B Small Perimeters

**1.** Position ruler following step 1 in Cutting A Small Corners on scrap or 8" square.

**2.** Mark along the smaller arc (Figure 4a). **Do not cut on this line.** Cut approximately ¼" inside the drawn arc referring to Figure 4b. Discard cutaway corner leaving B small perimeter piece (Figure 5).

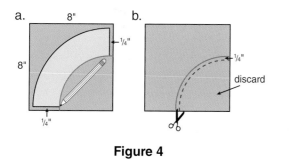

**Figure 4**

**Figure 5**

## Cutting C Large Corners

**1.** Position the ruler on the wrong side of a scrap or across the corner of a 10" square, leaving a ¼" seam allowance on each side of the straight edges referring again to Figure 1.

**2.** Draw along the larger arc of the ruler. **Do not cut on this line.** Cut approximately ½" outside the drawn arc referring to Figure 6.

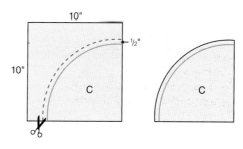

**Figure 6**

**3.** If using 10" squares, trim the square to 8" as shown in Figure 3 and then follow instructions in Cutting D Large Perimeters.

## Cutting D Large Perimeters

**1.** Position ruler following step 1 in Cutting A Small Corners on scrap or 8" square.

**2.** Mark along the larger arc (Figure 7a). **Do not cut on this line.** Cut approximately ¼" inside the drawn arc referring to Figure 7b. Discard cutaway corner leaving D large perimeter piece (Figure 8).

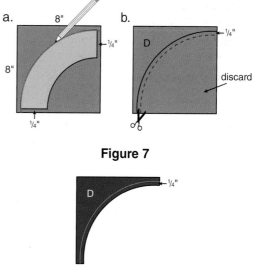

**Figure 7**

**Figure 8**

## Completing the Blocks

**1.** Clip curved seam allowance of every B and D perimeter piece. Press seam allowances toward wrong side of fabric along the marked line.

**2.** Position a C batik corner piece on right side of a D perimeter piece matching the stitching lines. Glue-baste and allow glue to dry, or pin pieces together at ends and center of seam and generously in between (Figure 9).

**Figure 9**

> **Designer's Tip**
>
> *Glue-baste the curved edges seam allowances together. Apply temporary fabric glue to the corner seam allowance. Position one end and then roll the corner piece down along the perimeter curve to the other end, pressing into place and matching the curved edges.*

**3.** Stitch together along the marked line ½" from piece edges.

**4.** Referring to the Assembly Diagram and Figure 10 for color combinations, repeat steps 2 and 3 to make a total of 32 Large Arch blocks.

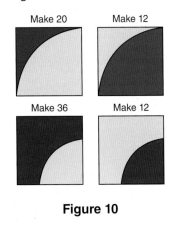

Make 20    Make 12

Make 36    Make 12

**Figure 10**

**5.** Referring to the Assembly Diagram and Figure 10 for color combinations, repeat steps 2 and 3 with A small corner and B small perimeter pieces to make 48 Small Arch blocks.

## Completing the Quilt

**1.** Arrange blocks in 10 rows of eight blocks each as shown in Figure 11; stitch blocks together in rows as arranged.

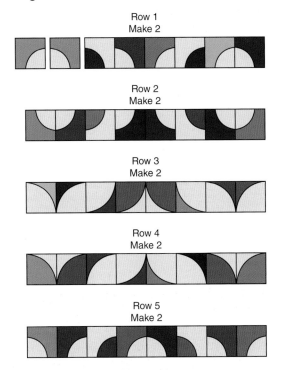

Row 1
Make 2

Row 2
Make 2

Row 3
Make 2

Row 4
Make 2

Row 5
Make 2

**Figure 11**

**2.** Arrange rows referring to the Assembly Diagram and stitch together, pressing seams in opposite directions in adjacent rows.

**3.** Stitch E/F strips together to make one long strip; press seams open.

**4.** Subcut strip into two each 1½" x 75½" E and 1½" x 62½" F border strips. Stitch E strips to sides and F strips to top and bottom of quilt center. Press seams toward borders.

**4.** Stitch G to sides of quilt and H to top and bottom referring to the Assembly Diagram to complete quilt center; press seams toward borders.

**5.** Sandwich the batting between the pieced top and a prepared backing piece; baste layers together. Quilt as desired.

**6.** When quilting is complete, remove basting, and trim batting and backing fabric even with raw edges of the pieced top.

**7.** Prepare binding and stitch to quilt front edges, matching raw edges, mitering corners and overlapping ends. Fold binding to back side and stitch in place to finish. ●

*"Ornamental Arches is made up of two different Drunkard's Path blocks, arranged in an elegant pattern that brings to mind the intricate carvings of the Moorish palace Alhambra in Granada, Spain." —Amy Krasnansky*

**Ornamental Arches**
Assembly Diagram 72" x 87"

# Ragged Mums

Designed & Quilted by Angie Buckles

The Double Wedding Ring Single Arc ruler makes fast and easy work of the petals on this ragged mum. This technique is sure to be a favorite.

## Skill Level
Confident Beginner

## Finished Size
Quilt Size: 52" x 66"

## Materials
- ½ yard 6 coordinating colors
- 4 yards gray tonal
- Backing to size
- Batting to size
- Thread
- Double Wedding Ring Single Arc ruler by EZ Quilting
- Basic sewing tools and supplies

## Project Notes
Read all instructions before beginning this project.

Stitch right sides together using a ¼" seam allowance unless otherwise specified.

Refer to a favorite quilting guide for specific techniques.

Materials and cutting lists assume 40" of usable fabric width.

## Cutting
Refer to General Instructions for Double Wedding Ring Single Arc ruler on page 7 for specific cutting instructions.

### From coordinating colors:
- Using the Double Wedding Ring Single Arc ruler, cut as many arcs as possible from each color.

### From gray tonal:
- Cut 2 (66½" by fabric width) strips.
  Subcut strips into 1 (21¼" x 66½") A rectangle and 1 (31¼" x 66½") B rectangle.

## Completing the Quilt
**1.** Stitch A and B rectangles together along length to make a 52½" x 66½" quilt top.

**2.** Sandwich the batting between the top and a prepared backing piece; baste layers together. Quilt as desired. Sample was quilted with a pattern of large leaves.

**3.** Following Placement Diagram, mark placement lines for arcs on quilt top.

**4.** Starting with the outer row of each mum, pin arcs in place, mixing colors and overlapping edges as desired.

**5.** Stitch on the inner curved edge only to sew the arcs in place.

**6.** Pin the next row of arcs in place, mixing colors and extending the placement of the arc so it covers the sewn-arcs stitching lines by at least ½".

**7.** Stitch in place.

**8.** Repeat placing, pinning and sewing each row of arcs in place working toward the center of each mum.

**9.** Insert other arcs as needed to add color or fill in open areas. Manipulate arcs by folding the inner curved edge or by pulling the bottom edge straight to cause the top edge to ruffle.

**10.** Fold or gather an arc to create the center of a mum and stitch in place.

## Binding the Quilt

This quilt can either be bound traditionally or a facing binding may be applied.

**1.** To bind traditionally, cut 2½" wide straight-of-grain strips from leftover gray tonal. Prepare binding and stitch to quilt front edges, matching raw edges, mitering corners and overlapping ends. Fold binding to back side and stitch in place to finish.

**2.** To apply a facing binding, cut 2" wide bias strips from leftover gray tonal. Refer to Facing Bindings on page 71 for detailed directions.

**3.** Wash quilt to rag raw edges of mums. ●

*"Mums, asters and zinnias are some of my favorite flowers. They're sturdy yet still soft, puffy and cozy. In this quilt, the arcs echo the rainbow of colors found in nature. After washing, they soften and become cozier." —Angie Buckles*

**Ragged Mums**
Placement Diagram 52" x 66"

# Facing Bindings

There are other binding options than the traditional single- or double-fold binding when that type of binding would detract from the overall design of the quilt. You could choose a backing self-binding with mitered corners or butted corners, knife-edge self-binding or facing binding.

Facing bindings made from strips with mitered corners or made from one piece of cloth are appropriate for small quilted pieces. The following adaptation made with strips works well for larger quilts.

**1.** Cut enough 2" wide bias or straight-grain strips from backing fabric to equal the circumference of the quilt plus 20".

**2.** Stitch strips together with angled seams; trim seam allowances to ¼" and press open. Subcut two strips each the measured lengths of the top/bottom and sides of the quilt plus 5".

**3.** Fold and press the strips in half wrong sides together. Stitch strips to quilt centered on top and bottom using a ¼" seam allowance. Backstitch at both ends to secure stitching.

**4.** Steam-press seam allowances toward binding and understitch seam allowances to binding (Photo A). **Note:** Understitching should be done as close to the seam as possible. This will help the front of the quilt to "roll" to the back of the quilt when the binding is folded to the back and secured.

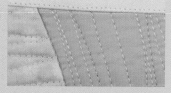
Photo A

**5.** Trim binding strips even with quilt top side edges.

**6.** Repeat steps 3 and 4 with side bindings. Trim side binding ends at an angle to quilt top edges. Fold side bindings to quilt wrong side referring to Photo B; steam-press, pin in place and hand-stitch to wrong side of quilt.

Photo B

**7.** Fold and steam-press top and bottom strip raw ends at an angle to wrong side (Photo C).

Photo C

**8.** Fold top strip to wrong side of quilt and pin in place (Photo D).

Photo D

**9.** Hand-stitch facing binding to back of quilt to secure, being sure to stitch corner folds in place (Photo E).

Photo E

# Arcs Bed Runner

Design by Nancy Scott
Quilted by Masterpiece Quilting

You won't believe how easy it can be to make this trendy Wedding Ring bed runner using a ruler and a bit of fusible appliqué.

## Skill Level
Confident Beginner

## Finished Size
Bed Runner Size: 80" x 40"
Block Size: 10" x 10"
Number of Blocks: 16

## Materials
- 1⅛ yards white solid
- 2 yards teal tonal
- 2⅔ yards gray tonal
- Paper-backed fusible web
- Backing to size
- Batting to size
- Thread
- Decorative variegated thread (optional)
- Basic sewing tools and supplies

## Project Notes
Read all instructions before beginning this project.

Stitch right sides together using a ¼" seam allowance unless otherwise specified.

Refer to a favorite quilting guide for specific techniques.

Materials and cutting lists assume 40" of usable fabric width.

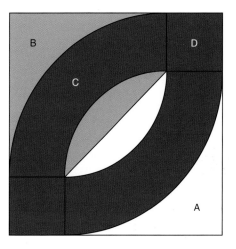

**Arcs**
10" x 10" Finished Block
Make 16

## Cutting
Refer to General Instructions for Double Wedding Ring Single Arc ruler on page 7 for specific cutting instructions.

### From white solid:
- Cut 3 (11" by fabric width) strips.
  Subcut strips into 8 (11") A squares.

### From teal tonal:
- Cut 7 (2½" by fabric width) binding strips.
- Cut 1 (36" by fabric width) strip for C arc appliqués.
- Cut 1 (9" by fabric width) D strip.

## From gray tonal:

- Cut 1 (88" by fabric width) strip.
  Subcut strip lengthwise into 2 (10" x 80") E strips.
  Cut remainder of strip lengthwise into
    1 (11" x 88") strip. Subcut into 8 (11") B squares.

## Preparing the Arc Appliqués

**1.** Fuse paper-backed fusible web to wrong side of D strip, following manufacturer's directions and Raw-Edge Fusible Applique on page 61. Subcut into 32 (3") D squares. Do not remove paper.

**2.** Trace 32 arc shapes onto paper side of fusible web.

**3.** Following manufacturer's directions, apply fusible web with traced arc shapes onto wrong side of the 36" by fabric width strip of teal tonal.

**4.** Cut out 32 C arcs on traced lines. Do not remove paper.

## Completing the Blocks

**1.** Draw a diagonal line on wrong side of each white square.

**2.** Layer an A square on a B square and stitch ¼" on either side of the marked line. Cut on drawn line and press seam toward B. Repeat to make 16 A-B units referring to Figure 1.

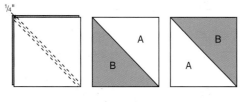

**Figure 1**

**3.** Position two C arcs fusible side down on an A-B unit 3" from corners and ¼" from edges as shown in Figure 2; fuse in place following manufacturer's instructions. Repeat with all C arcs and A-B units.

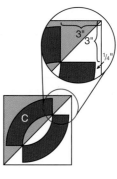

**Figure 2**

**4.** Machine-stitch all C arcs in place on concave and convex curves using desired decorative stitch.

**5.** Position and fuse two D squares in corners of C arcs referring to Figure 3. Machine-appliqué sides of each square catching ends of C arcs to complete a block.

**Figure 3**

**6.** Repeat step 5 to complete 16 Arcs blocks.

## Completing the Quilt

**1.** Following the Assembly Diagram for color orientation, sew blocks into two rows; press seams in opposite directions.

**2.** Sew rows together matching points referring again to the Assembly Diagram; press.

**3.** Sew E borders onto top and bottom of center section, press seams toward E.

**4.** Sandwich the batting between the pieced top and a prepared backing piece; baste layers together. Quilt as desired.

**5.** When quilting is complete, remove basting, and trim batting and backing fabric even with raw edges of the pieced top.

**6.** Prepare binding and stitch to quilt front edges, matching raw edges, mitering corners and overlapping ends. Fold binding to back side and stitch in place to finish. ●

*"By just using the arcs, you get the look of a Double Wedding Ring without all the work. This bed runner gives you lots of flexibility to personalize it. You can change the number of rings to adjust the length and alter the width of the outer borders to create a custom fit for your bed." —Nancy Scott*

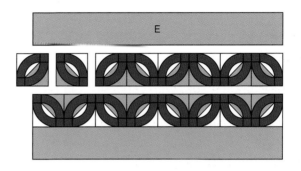

**Arcs Bed Runner**
Assembly Diagram 80" x 40"

# Round Up the Squares

### Designed & Quilted by Amy Krasnansky

## Looking for a new and exciting way to do Wedding Ring quilts? You've just found it.

## Skill Level

Intermediate

## Finished Size

Quilt Size: 46" x 63"

## Materials

- ⅜ yard coral/aqua batik
- 1¼ yards aqua batik
- 1¾ yards light coral batik
- 2 yards dark coral batik
- 2¾ yards medium coral batik
- Backing to size
- Batting to size
- Thread
- Monofilament thread
- Freezer paper
- Temporary fabric glue
- Double Wedding Ring ruler by EZ Quilting
- Basic sewing tools and supplies

## Project Notes

Read all instructions before beginning this project.

Stitch right sides together using a ¼" seam allowance unless otherwise specified.

Refer to a favorite quilting guide for specific techniques.

Materials and cutting lists assume 40" of usable fabric width.

## Cutting

Refer to General Instructions for Double Wedding Ring Single Arc ruler on page 7 for specific cutting instructions.

## From coral/aqua batik:

- Cut 2 (4¾" by fabric width) strips.
    Subcut strips into 6 (2⅝" x 4¾") D rectangles and 8 (4¾") C squares.
    Trim remainder of strip to 2⅝" and subcut strip into 4 (2⅝") E squares.

## From aqua batik:

- Cut 6 (2½" by fabric width) binding strips.
- Cut 5 (8" by remaining fabric length) strips.
    Subcut strips into 5 arcs from 4 strips and 4 arcs from the remaining strip for a total of 24 B arcs referring to Figure 1 and using Double Wedding Ring Single Arc ruler.

**Figure 1**

## From dark coral batik:

- Cut 4 (5½" by fabric length) strips.
    Subcut strips into 2 each 5½" x 53½" H and 5½" x 48" I borders.

## Designer's Tip

*The intended finished outer border size is 5", but strips can be cut up to 6" wide and slightly longer to ensure that the quilt can be squared up and trimmed to match the appliqué overlay.*

**From medium coral batik:**
- Cut 6 (1" by fabric width) F/G strips.
- Cut 5 (8" by remaining fabric length) strips. Subcut strips into 5 arcs from 4 strips and 4 arcs from the remaining strip for a total of 24 A arcs referring again to Figure 1.

## Completing the Appliqué Overlay

**1.** Prepare several freezer-paper templates by tracing around the single arc ruler onto the dull side of freezer paper (Figure 2a). Cut out pieces and trim away the ¼" seam allowance (Figure 2b).

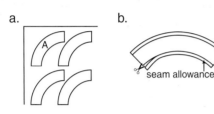

seam allowance

**Figure 2**

## Determining Border Lengths

- *To measure for straight borders, lay the pieced quilt top on a flat surface.*

- *Measure the quilt top through the center from top to bottom and add ½" for seams.*

- *Measure the quilt top through the center from side to side. Add twice the width of the border plus ½" for seams to this measurement to determine the length to cut the top and bottom borders.*

- *If making mitered borders, add at least twice the border width to side, top and bottom border lengths and refer to mitered border instructions for construction.*

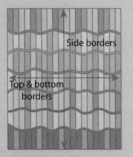

**Measuring for Border Lengths**

**2.** Iron the shiny side of an arc template centered onto the wrong side of a fabric arc.

**3.** Press seam allowances of fabric curved edges over the freezer-paper template (Figure 3); carefully remove the freezer paper and reuse. Clip the concave arc seam allowance.

**Figure 3**

**4.** Stitch two A arcs, curving away from each other, onto one side of a C square leaving ¼" seam allowances on the edges of the square as shown in Figure 4. Press seams toward C.

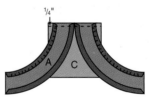

**Figure 4**

**5.** Repeat step 4 with two more A arcs on opposite side of C; press seams toward C.

**6.** Repeat steps 4 and 5 with B arcs on remaining sides of C (Figure 5).

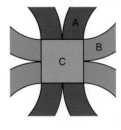

**Figure 5**